Find Your Hustle: How to Double Your Income With a Side Gig

Immanuel Byoma

Table of Content

Introduction

Introduction

A lot has been said and taught about side hustles already. Chances are you already have one, but is it the right one for you?

Not all side hustles were created equal. Some have the potential to transform your life beyond finances and move you from a place of debt, frustration, and obscurity to a realm of wealth, peace and nobility – you will stand before kings and queens.

'Find your hustle' is about helping you locate the one that was made for you; or rather, you were made for. By doing it, you will be able to double your income in as little as one year. This is not about getting rich quick, but rather finding your Pareto advantage and leveraging the 80/20 principle.

There has always been something you do better than most, now is the time to turn that into a side hustle and thrive!

The primary principle of this book is this: **nobody should have a side hustle, instead everyone should have a side flow**. A side flow is the next step up from a side hustle and it is guaranteed to change your life.

Over the past four years, I have earned more from my hustles as a content marketer and consultant than from my day job. Not only do I earn more from my side gigs, but I also enjoy them a lot more.

Now, is your time to find a hustle you will thoroughly enjoy and will help you make a huge leap forward financially, emotionally, socially and maybe even physically (beware of the extra dough).

Here's to a new chapter in your life (pun intended).

Chapter 1: Why You Need A Side Hustle

There are two ways to make a living: the stressed way or the blessed way.

The stressed way is what most people do: you go to work every day, slave away and put up with a lot of trash from your superiors because you know you can't do without the job or rather, the money. It is not very productive. You wait and hope for a raise each year and you bitch about your boss if you don't get it.

The blessed way: you go to work, grind all day long and you love what you do. You are working the same hours, sometimes even longer, but you believe in what you do. You realise that the work is the reward, not the money, even though you are well compensated. Because you throw your heart into what you do and you do it with a good attitude, you are constantly experiencing growth.

If you don't know what that feels like, you need a side hustle desperately. Most people hate their jobs or bosses, but everybody wants to make money. So, naturally, when people consider side hustles, they think about how much money they can make. But that's putting the cart before the horse.

If you think only about the money, your foresight will be limited. You will miss out on REAL opportunities. There are many reasons why you need a side hustle and yes money is one of them, but it is not the main one.

A side hustle is meant to help you achieve higher levels of success.

By success, I mean: you are ahead of your bills, you live in a good house which you own or will eventually own, you can take care of your family, send your kids to good schools/universities and have a personal life. You are thriving, not merely surviving.

Here are some other reasons why you need a side hustle:

1. To find your comparative advantage

How good are you at your job? How much do you earn compared to people in your industry? Are you a top performer or are you just okay? If you're great or not, it's not a problem.

If you're one of the best in your field, then you have already found your comparative advantage and that's what you need to explore further with your side hustle. If you're not (and most of us aren't), then you owe it to yourself to discover it.

Your comparative advantage is what you do better than 80% of other people with equal or more training and experience. It's something that comes to you naturally and you are excellent at.

The reason you can discover this easier with a side hustle than with a regular job is that a job is something you use to pay the bills, while the side hustle is something you use to express your talents/skills/abilities.

Many people work jobs they hate because the income is good. Don't do the same with your side hustle. Choose something you enjoy, that you're passionate about. If you can't narrow it down to one thing, then try several of them and see which one sticks.

While this may not pay as much money immediately, you will soon rise to the top of your game in a few years and then you'll be a baller.

2. To diversify your income

The world is a fickle place. One day, you have the best job, the next day your company is bankrupt. How do you protect against such shocks?

You do so by getting money on the side. Now, if your job is paying you $2,000 a month and your side hustle pulls in just $200, you have no real protection, do you?

This is why it is vitally important that you pick something you are very good at because the rate of increase is geometric, not arithmetic. Arithmetic is addition, geometric is multiplication. This is your year to multiply.

Remember, of course, that the goal isn't simply to make as much money as possible today. If that was the case, then the best strategy would be to get a job that pays more and forget this talk about side hustles.

What you need is an alternative source of income that will protect you just in case one goes down. In my case, I have three main sources of income. Each one of these can cover all of my routine costs. I also have two smaller ones. To grow further, I have to turn my side hustles into a company, and I'll be hiring full-time staff to help me share the load.

This leads me to my next point.

3. A side hustle is a soft entry into entrepreneurship

Have you ever wanted to be an entrepreneur but found the process scary? Maybe you wonder "what if it doesn't work?" What if after you quit your job, you find out your business idea is a bust?

Roughly 60% of adults want to be their own boss, but only 4% are. Why is that? The reality of it is frightening, especially if you have a family to look after, bills, or a comfortable lifestyle you would like to maintain.

So, instead of jumping head in, start with a side hustle. Take your time to develop your side hustle until it can stand on its own. This way, you don't forfeit the security of your full-time job, and you have also taken the time to ascertain the profitability of your business.

4. A side hustle gives you financial freedom

A wise man said '**Sow your seed** in the morning, and at evening let not **your** hands be idle, for you do not know which will succeed, whether this or that, or whether both will do equally well.'

My interpretation – go to work in the morning, then run your side hustle in the evening. You don't know which one will perform better! Sure, your salary might pay you a lot more now, but if you can develop your hustle, that could change soon.

Not only can a side hustle provide a good side income, but it can also actually become your main source of income by a country mile.

The same wise man also said, "invest in seven or eight things, because you don't know what evil may befall the land."

Investing wisely is the greatest side hustle. Every expert will tell you to always diversify your portfolio. No matter how good a stock is, it can let you down. However, it is unlikely for all the good stocks to crash at the same time.

Don't leave financial freedom up to chance, and don't assume it is something you can never obtain. The idea that you will always be in debt, would never be wealthy, or you would struggle in retirement are all lies!

Many people have found their best lives via their side hustles and I need you to be one of them. I believe it can happen for you and so should you.

Chapter 2: What Can Be A Side Hustle?

The Webster definition of a side hustle (kidding, this is my definition) is any job you do that is in the informal sector i.e. you work without a formal contract of employment. Having a second job is not a side hustle, it's a second job. I don't want that for you.

I don't even want you to have a side hustle; I want you to have a side flow.

A hustle is hard work, stress, frustration, and disappointment. A flow is a steady stream of clients, jobs, prospects, income, and delight. It's a stage in your life where everything just seems to click.

Before now, when you thought about a side hustle, you imagined something basic that doesn't require much intellect, right? You think about Airbnb, Uber, laundry service, washing cars, selling lemonade in summer. These are all great things and every one of them can give you something extra. But there is more to side hustles than these.

A side hustle is anything someone can pay you for. It could be a blog that gets you paid via ad sense. It could be a karate class for adults you hold in your basement. It can be a band, a comedy skit, teaching make-up, writing books, running errands, etc.

There are no boundaries, but there are rules. For example, Chris Guillebeau, author of the book *Side Hustle*, says that Uber is not a side hustle. Why not? Because you are working for someone who determines how much you get paid.

A side hustle should give you flexibility and unlimited room for growth. What I say, however, is that if your dream is to own a taxi service or a fleet of cars under Uber, then yes, it is your side hustle and that could be your comparative advantage. Unlike all the other drivers, you have a vision. You see a result much bigger than what lies in front of you and you're ready to take it. You're not just driving the car, you are studying the market. Learning about customer interactions and satisfaction. You are picking up more than fares; you're accumulating life lessons that will one day help you run your own service.

If I just gave you an idea, I want copyright! Kidding.....not really.

Don't be limited in your perception of side hustles, especially of how far they can take you.

My side hustle started as freelance writing. With that, I have been able to learn my way into becoming a digital marketing consultant. But you know who I always envied? Web designers! They get paid wayyy more than I do and their job looks cool.

Then you have the people that are fashion designers, dog-walkers, graphic designers, YouTube stars, social media influencers and all sorts of different things.
A lot of singers act as their side hustle, and a lot of actors sing as side hustles and some even win Grammy Awards (dang you, Bradley!!!).

One of the best side hustles for professionals is being a consultant. If you love your career or have learnt a lot about a certain aspect of your career and you are a leader in that field, you can be a consultant.

This is the side hustle I recommend for everyone. As a consultant, you get paid a lot of money not to work. You are paid to teach other people how to work. You are hired by companies and corporations in desperate need to fix problems and they are willing to pay thousands of dollars.

A lot of public speakers are consultants, with some clocking as much as $50,000 per hour to teach. Would you call that a hustle or a flow? After just one hour of work, they make more than 90% of the working population in the world! Do you know what that means? It means that 90% of the roughly 3 billion working adults in the world make less than many public speakers and consultants do in an hour! I know that's just me repeating myself, but you have to understand just what it means to have an EPIC side flow.

We're not talking about athletes or superstars with freakish talents they have developed since they were in the womb. I'm talking about regular people that are good at their jobs and know how to address an audience, making more than 2.7 billion people do…in an hour!

I'm not saying this to depress you, but to stimulate you. You can be a top earner like that, and sooner than you think.

You may not be a public speaker, but if you can teach groups of people how to excel at something important, you can be a consultant. Instead of making that money an hour, you can make it in four weekends of training corporate leaders. Not bad, no?

Of course, for you to get to this level, you must have first proven yourself in a particular field. The best part is it doesn't matter what field it is. You can be a hairstylist and get paid a lot to teach other hairstylists. You can be a farmhand, a manicurist, an artisanal soap maker or a DJ. It doesn't matter. The only thing that matters is that you are very good at it.

Another great side hustle is real estate. Real estate has made more millionaires than any other industry in history. If you live in a county with a developed real estate market and a healthy credit market, you can do some serious work here.

As good as all of these things sound, it is not okay for you to roll dice before you choose one. These are all side hustles, but they can't all be *your* side hustle, and that my friend, is the most important thing to learn from this book.

Chapter 3: Discovering Your Side Hustle

There are a million websites with lists of 100 or 250 things you can do as a side hustle. I have mentioned a few of them above, but it is an unending list.

However, we are looking for your comparative advantage – the thing that will make you stand out from the crowd and earn WAYYY more than anything you are doing right now. Do you honestly see yourself retiring early from being a Lyft driver? Do you see yourself fulfilling your dream of traveling around the world as a graphic artist, painter or singer?

If the answer for you is 'no', then you need to find your 'yes'. Don't just throw yourself at anything and hope for the best.

One year from now, you could be earning twice as much as you are now. I know it sounds ridiculous, but if I hadn't seen countless people that did it and if I hadn't done it myself, maybe I would think it was impossible too. It took me a long road to get this, but it doesn't have to take that much time for you.

There is a system you can employ to help you achieve that goal that involves knowing what you want, having the right mindset and leveraging on your side hustle. Let's face it, no matter how good you are at your job, it's unlikely your boss will double your salary. If you get a 30% raise that would be huge. With that 30% increase, it means all you have to get from your side hustle is the remaining 70%. If you choose your side gig wisely, you would be able to replicate that success the following year.

Why is that? There is no limit to how much your side hustle can pay. There is no salary cap or company policy that will prevent you from earning your fair dues. The only thing that can stop your earnings from your side hustle is you.

Case Study

Let's say you are a fantastic dancer and you start teaching dance lessons in your basement once a week. You start with 5 students for free. If you are as good as you think, then by the end of the month you could have 20 people paying you $20 a month for one-hour classes every Thursday evening, which is very low. But now you're making $400 extra each month.

How do you grow from there? Simple: add another day. If you can get an extra 10 people for the second day, then you now have $600 extra each month. Besides this, you can get private clients that will pay you $20-$40 an hour, especially couples about to get married. If you do just ten hours of this every month, that's an extra $200-$400.

Now you've got maybe $1,000 extra each month. Is there any rule that says you can't teach dance seven days a week? Is there any policy stopping you from charging $100 an hour or $20/hour for a class of 10-15 people? No!

Again, if you are as good as you think, this could mean you're making $200 per hour in 3-6 months. Calculate how many hours you will need to double your income. That's just year one.

In year two, you can start a YouTube channel, a dancing website, sell dance instruction videos on your website or a platform like Udemy, whatever! You can quit your day job and teach it full time. Before you know it, you could double your income again the second year!

By year 3, you are in such high demand you have to charge more for your classes, and your dance videos are selling out quickly and your website/vlog is also getting you passive income from affiliate marketing, Google ads, and other sponsored posts.

Not only does this sound great, but it is an experience many people have had, some with even more astounding success than that.

But this is my question for you – do you know anything about dancing? If you have two left feet like me, then chances are you won't even make a dollar as a dance instructor, and you would then feel discouraged and say "side hustles don't work."

Not true!

They work, you just happened to choose the WRONG side hustle. You chose one that could never become your side flow. However, if you are good at marketing, then you could be the one that sets up the website and social media channels for the dance instructor and many others like him and make your money that way.

The only person that can limit your income from side hustling is you. That is such an empowering feeling. You get to decide your income – after you have mastered it of course, and within reason. It might be possible to make a million dollars a month as a dance instructor, but maybe not without a business, a best-selling book or a million followers.

Here's the fun thing about wealth and success though: there is no one way to do it. You can achieve phenomenal success as easily from being a high-powered investment broker as you can being a pig farmer, a fashion designer, masseuse, hairstylist, manicurist, dog trainer or realtor.

It depends on one major thing: your gift. Whatever you are gifted at and you develop diligently, will give you an equal chance of success as anyone else, and this is why:

The 80/20 Principle

The 80/20 principle has a lot of interpretations. It is also known as the Pareto principle or Pareto advantage. It says that 80 percent of your productivity is the result of 20 percent of your effort. A Pareto advantage is also something you do better than 80 percent of people.

Now, in every field on earth without exception, the top performers are millionaires or billionaires. At the very least, the top twenty percent, therefore, rake in hundreds of thousands of dollars a year. I just read about a guy who makes six-figures picking up trash. Not recycling, picking up. He doesn't pick up lost treasure, trash! And he said anyone can do it because there is enough trash to go around. If he's right (which I bet he is) then even trash pickers can become millionaires.

The top 20% in any field make 80% of the money, the same way 80% of the land in any country is owned by the wealthiest 20%. If you want to crack that list, you need to find the thing you do better than 80 percent of people. Not 5% or even 50% of people, but 80.

Another way to see this is that it is something you can do in an hour what would take others four hours to do. You do in two hours what would take others eight hours to do.

Can you see where this is going? This is how you can double your income: you are so productive that your two hours of hustling after work each day will get you the same as your eight hours at work. Or five hours on Saturday and five hours on Sunday.

Wowza! What are you waiting for?

I'm guessing you have not discovered your PDC yet. Honestly, you probably do, but you've just not had the faith or confidence to believe it and work on it. So, let's dig a little deeper and discover it together. I really want you to get this. This is your ticket out of whatever financial hole you're in, or into whatever financial haven you want to get into.

This is your way out of broke, bad bosses and boredom. This is your way into a life and job you thoroughly enjoy and rewards you like a criminal. Okay, bad metaphor, but you get the idea.

Let's dive right in.

How to discover your comparative advantage/gift/Pareto advantage/awesomeness

For simplicity, I'm going to refer to your comparative advantage as PDC. It means purpose/destiny/calling. It is your God-given ability that will set you apart from everybody else. It is your basketball to Michael Jordan, wrestling to Hulk Hogan, Tennis to Federer & Serena, acting to Samuel L. Jackson, talk-show hosting to Steve Harvey, compassion to Mother Theresa, computer wizardry to Bill Gates and singing to Celine Dion.

You can't teach this stuff from nothing. There has to be something inside you that is then worked on, developed and unleashed like a wild banshee. You are born with it, but you need some help getting it out.
If you have never known your gift before now, I need you to answer just a few questions:

1. What do you do (any action whatsoever, not necessarily work-related) that always gets compliments?
2. What did you dream of becoming as a child?
3. Which problem do you see that always bothers you and nags at you, calling you to do something about it?
4. What would you gladly do for free to satisfy your passion?
5. What would you die for?

In all likelihood, your answer to the first question is your PDC. Your PDC isn't something you have to tell people, they know it. You don't have to convince people you're funny; if nobody laughs, you're not funny! If people turn away when you sing, you can't!

For a long time, I could not accept that writing was one of my PDC's (oh yeah, you can have multiple, like The Rock or Oprah or Barack Obama). I was a very insecure person growing up, so I never thought much of myself. I rejected compliments because I thought people were making fun of me.

When someone said to me a few years ago that what I wrote for his magazine was better than most of the people on Forbes and time Magazine, I thought he was talking trash. So, I guess this is an important side lesson – you have to be willing to hear the truth.

Insecurity is deadly. It can cripple you before you begin and prevent you from becoming who you were meant to be.

My fiancé tried convincing me for years that I was a good writer. Fiancé. The most important person in my life and I didn't believe her. See how crazy low self-esteem can be? When I eventually did two years ago, I started seeing radical results. Before that, the money was trickling in, but now it's a lot more.

Did that knowledge make me a better writer? No, it didn't, but it made me value my work more. Now, I am paid almost double what I accepted before because I know the worth of my work.

Maybe you are currently accepting very little from your present employer because you don't know how valuable you are, and your boss probably won't tell you unless you threaten to quit.

Fun exercise: if you think your job is your PDC, apply to other companies and find out what they are willing to offer you. If you get better offers, then you are right and it is your PDC. If you don't, it's not.

I did not say you should quit your job, I said 'fun exercise'. However, if you do get a better job offer and you think it's right for you, take it! I did that earlier this year and it was great, although I just wanted to leave my job. Before that though, something just as startling happened.

A company was looking for a part-time social media manager. Because my side hustles were going fine, I was open to the position. When they told me what they were offering I nearly turned it down – it was half of my salary at the time. However, I was able to sell myself to the HR manager and not only did I get the job as a consultant instead of a part-time employer, but they also offered me six times more!

That is a lesson in knowing your value and I am grateful to my fiancé for that.

Do you have someone in your life that knows you inside and out and that can tell you for certain what your PDC is? Maybe your spouse, parents, best friend, colleague, kids or postal officer? Whoever it is, ask them what they think and look into it.

What you find might pleasantly surprise you, and maybe make you feel foolish for being underpaid for years. Once you have the answer, it is time to turn it into gold.

Do not say you are too young or too old. Don't be afraid of people. Don't be afraid of failure, because failure is afraid of you. You cannot fail at your PDC, it is impossible. The only way to fail is to not do it. Once you start, you will see everything begin to fall in place for you. Strangers will want to help you. Opportunities will seem to appear all of a sudden. The same people you hang around will remember someone they know that needs the services you are offering.

How do I know? Because it happens to me. It has happened to all the successful people on earth and it will happen to you. But first, you have to do something with your talents. Do something with it, anything, and watch it multiply. Fact.

Here is another fact for you: if you don't discover your PDC or fail to apply it, you will regret it for the rest of your life. Now, that's failure and I'm not going to let that happen to you.

It's time to launch out into the deep and unleash your side hustle.

Chapter 4: Unleashing Your Side Hustle

It is not enough to know your PDC, you have to put it to good use. Emphasis on good use – a drug dealer is not a PDC. Marketing probably is, but drug dealing is not!

Before you begin, I need you to have a long-term view. You can either be a flash of brilliant light, or an eternal ray of sunshine. A lot of people have tried a side hustle, gotten paid, but never translated it into anything worthwhile or long-lasting. They only saw what was right in front of their noses.

When you discover your PDC, you should be prepared to nurture and develop it for the rest of your life. Your immediate desire, therefore, is to watch it germinate. It doesn't have to become a huge tree overnight. You need time for your roots to sink deep down into good soil, so you grow consistently over time and can withstand any economic shocks.

It is a marathon, but you are going to sprint all the way when you know your gifts. Point is, however, don't be eager for quick gains.

Here are the steps for you to unleash your side hustle:

1.   Take time to develop it

Money should not be your primary motivator; your talent should be. The first thing you want to do is prove that you have indeed identified your PDC. You do this by taking on small jobs. Don't go big just yet. Look for freelance opportunities that pay you little or nothing.

Do this for 1-3 months. Take the time to just see how good you are, learn the ropes and study the market.

Join a few platforms online that will allow you to experiment with your gifts. There are great sites for freelancing such as peopleperhour and Fiverr, websites for coaching and consulting such as clarity.fm, ride-sharing apps, websites for chores and also for tutoring. Whatever you want to do, there is probably a platform somewhere you can experiment with.

Be patient if you don't see immediate results. You might not get your first client immediately but stick with it. Learn how to pitch yourself, organise your time, haggle and interact with clients.

This is an additional income, so you can afford to price yourself low, to begin with, if you don't have a track record. If you are consulting and you already have an established career, then you might have connections that will help you get good opportunities straight away.

The same thing if you have been building websites for fun and now want to do it for others. If you have proof of success already, then you can begin at a higher price point, but don't be greedy or arrogant.

Be prepared to earn very little for the first few months as you develop your gift, website, and social media presence.

2. Find a mentor

Mentorship is priceless. People often ask if you need a mentor to succeed. Truth is you don't, but it makes it a lot easier.

I did not have a mentor when I started freelancing. If I did, I would have progressed a lot faster. I am mentoring a friend of mine at the moment and he is making a lot more than I was when I first started.

The mentor does not have to be someone you know personally. It could be someone in your field whose blog you subscribe to – mine are Neil Patel and Heather Lloyd-Martin, for content marketing. I have Brian Tracy and Jack Canfield for coaching, consulting and public speaking.

These mentors will share industry knowledge, trade secrets and give a lot of free advice to help you flourish. Please, take their advice seriously. It will help you avoid a lot of pitfalls and help you progress faster. Some of them could even help you compress a year's worth of progress into seven days, like Gary Ryan Blair.

If you know someone personally, that is even better. Find a mentor, and listen to them attentively.

3. Get excellent

Nobody can resist excellence. When people see something great, they are willing to pay a premium for it. Get as good as you can. Take courses, practice, take on different challenges. Don't limit yourself. If you get the opportunity to do things outside your comfort zone, go for it. Don't be afraid of hard work or complications.

When I started copywriting, I wasn't interested in SEO. I thought it was just a waste of time and too much effort. I just wanted to write. How foolish I was. If I had learnt SEO at the time, I would've been a much better writer a lot sooner. I eventually learnt it, but I missed out on doubling my fees quicker.

Don't be an idiot like I once was. Learn what you need to. Grow quickly. Crave feedback, whether positive or negative.

I remember writing for a company once that had a gut-puncher as the editor. His criticism was so harsh I wanted to spit in his coffee. I was doing this online, so we never met and I have no idea what he looks like.

After I got my senses back, I realised that his criticisms, as harsh as they were, helped me become a better writer. I credit a lot of my growth to that man that tore my writing to shreds.

Work for mean people. Do work for perfectionists, knowing that if you can please them, you can please anybody. Work with people that will be honest with their feedback. Let them tell you the truth. The truth will only make you better. Better yet, it will make you more excellent.

If you are not getting any positive reviews, then you know you picked the wrong side hustle. It's time to try something else.

If you are now a Rockstar, then it's time to get paid!

4. Study the market and set a good price

After you have grown your skills over the past few months, it's time to start thinking about fair wages. You have been paid pittance for 3-9 months and it has been totally worth it, I promise.

Every job has a trial period. After 3-6 months you get a performance review. If you have done well, you get to keep your job or even get a raise. It's the same thing with a side hustle, except you are the one giving yourself a raise and there is no cap.

Now it's time to do your research into the market. Find out what people earn based on their level of experience and skill. Dig into the companies or people that pay more for the type of service you offer. Consider your best marketing options and go for it.

For example, let's say you are a marketing consultant. Over the past 6 months, you have worked with twelve brands pro bono and you have helped some of them grow their income 30%. That's huge! As a consultant, you can charge 10% of that growth as commission, or even 20%.

The next company you go to, therefore, won't get your service for free. You can charge a flat figure or a commission – I like commissions because they are more challenging and rewarding.

Let's say the Soap store you go to sells $10,000 worth of product per month. You have studied them and realised they can do $20,000 a month. That's an increase of $10,000. You can charge them a 10% commission on whatever growth you help them achieve. Some companies would be happy to offer 30%.

Find out what works best and charge a fair price. Don't go under and don't go over. Don't milk the cow dry in other words. Charge a good price that will encourage referrals. You don't want companies to say 'Lucy is great, but she is too expensive.' There's nothing wrong with being pricey, but too expensive means you charge more than the value you give.

It's better to get referrals saying 'she is worth it!' That means you are expensive, but still below the value they received. With a couple of referrals, you'll find that you have met your doubling target.

Thumbs up!

5. Launch out into the deep

Realistically, you can expect to be earning the industry average by month 9. After getting a good wage for months 9-12, it is time to launch out into the deep and let down your nets.

Over the past year, you have developed your PDC, worked for a variety of clients – some good, some bad and some tried to steal from you, and you have grown. Over the past quarter, you started earning a good wage. Some of you have become millionaires already!

Nevertheless, whatever you have done up until now is child's play. It is time for the real work to begin.

Update your LinkedIn page, get a proper website if you want to and get business cards with your new title. This is assuming you're not already swamped with clients and you have the bandwidth to take on some more. You might be ready to even start a full-time business.

Now you are in a position to become a consultant, public speaker, thought leader or a mentor. You know enough to maybe write a book or at least start a blog to help other people.

Let me share with you the ultimate secret to success: put other people first. The more you want to help others, the more successful you will become. Fix your mind on solving problems for others. Don't be self-obsessed, be people-obsessed. Think day and night about how you can help others.

You might feel like you don't know enough to help others, but if you have successfully doubled your income by now via a combination of work and investments, then you know more than enough.

Don't take for granted your budding success. Share your tips and just maybe, that could turn into another income stream.

If you don't want a marquee gig that will take you away from your job, you can look for ways to earn more from your side hustles. Find even higher-paying clients, and look for ways to automate the process, so you are spending less time while making more.

Don't be satisfied with doubling your income one year, try and do it again the second year, and the third if possible. And it is; all things are possible to them who believe.

Chapter 5: How I Double My Income

There is a very simple formula I use to double my income each year and it's so simple in fact, many people doubt it.

All I do, to be honest, is say that my goal for the year is to double my income and it happens, with some help from 'the universe'. It's worked for the past couple of years. However, I got more than I expected this year. Within the first four months of the year, I had more than doubled my income.

I was in the process of trying to double it again when my attention was drawn to the plight of others. There I was, earning more than my former boss, complaining about how I wanted even more money when I realised that a few of my friends were struggling financially.

I felt so selfish. Things were going well for me, but I had not shared the secret with others. So, I took a break from trying to get more money to write this book. I do hope this book helps me exceed my income goals, but that is a side note. The real blessing would be helping other people achieve success and actualise their dreams.

So, here is the formula in more detail:

1. Say what you want – double your income in a specific year
2. Look for ways to make more money from your side hustle or by offering extra services
3. Find the opportunities and apply

I doubled my income this year by adding social media consultancy to my repertoire. It was something I could do, but not as well as content marketing. However, the opportunity came and I went for it.

As I shared earlier, the initial offer from the company was a lot lower than I expected. After I got their offer, I sent an email explaining why social media was important and why they should be willing to invest four times more than their current offer in a good social media manager.

They were convinced and they brought me on board (as a consultant) for even more than I initially said. After that, I got another full-time job that paid much more than my previous employer.

Saying that you want to double your income isn't enough, you need to back it up with actions. Take opportunities as they come. Seize the day. In both instances, the offers came to me. My former boss actually told me about the social media role, while a recruiter on LinkedIn asked if I was interested in a full-time job. I applied, interviewed and scaled through.

When you say things in faith, wonderful things happen. This is a phenomenon that can't be explained with logic. It just happens. If you're saying right now you don't think you can double your income, it probably won't happen. If you are afraid of looking foolish if it doesn't happen, be afraid instead of not finding out. Give it a shot! It has worked very well for me for the past few years. My fixed monthly earnings from work and consulting contracts (not including inconsistent writing opportunities) are ten times more than they were just three years ago.

As soon as I finish this book, I'll be sending out proposals to other companies. I will also be turning this book into a course on Udemy – lookout for it. I can afford to invest more time in trying to help other people find their side hustles because I have surpassed my income target for the year, so maybe I'll hold off on the proposals for now?

I must warn you though, that when you say you want to double your income people might think you're crazy or being unrealistic. I only told one person my plan for the year and she didn't think it was possible. However, telling her kept me accountable.

By sharing your vision, you are forced to stay true to your word. When you get the money, and I say when not if, you need to know how to make it multiply.

Chapter 6: What to Do With Your Extra Money

Before we get ahead of ourselves, there is something important you need to know: making a lot of money will not give you financial freedom. Earning millions of dollars a year will not guarantee that you retire a millionaire.

Many one-time millionaires are broker than people who never earned more than $50,000 a year. Heck, some are now even homeless.

Impossible? Mike Tyson, Dennis Rodman, Michael Jackson, Mozart. They earned a lot of money but spent it faster than they made it.

There is no point in doubling your income if you are just going to blow it. The money you make today should be handled wisely.

1. Save

There are different schools of thought on saving. The recommended minimum for a high earner is 20 percent. Saving 10 percent is okay, but with the extra cash you are making, you can afford to save more. Don't see your side hustle as part of your monthly earnings. This is money you would not have gotten and you would have been fine without it.

Jay Leno said that throughout his career, he always had two sources of income. He lived on the smaller one and saved the larger sum. As the host of 'The Tonight Show', he reportedly earned as much as $30 million a year. He saved all of that and lived off the money he earned doing stand-up comedy.

That is way more than saving 20%! There are no hard and fast rules, but what I try to do is save to achieve future goals. Look ahead and see what you would like to achieve, then figure out how much you need to save. For me right now, that means saving 60%.

2. Invest

Investment is the lifeblood of wealth. It is very hard to build wealth without investing. I don't pretend to be a master in investment, for that you need a qualified CPA, stockbroker, investment banker, CFA, etc.

What I do is invest in mutual funds, which are pretty safe, and land. I highly recommend buying stocks and bonds too and investing in your retirement fund.

Speak to a professional and find out your options. Investing allows your money work for you and compound interest is a gift from heaven! An example from Dave Ramsey showed that if you invest just $2,000 a year for 35 years in an investment fund that yields 12%, you will be a millionaire! I know it should be $70,000, but compound interest is wonderful. I'm pretty sure you can invest more than $2,000 a year, even though the interest rate might not be much higher.

3. Give

Contrary to popular opinion, generosity does not make you poor, it makes you wealthier. When you learn to give – to God, parents, family, charity – you unlock a higher level of creativity and productivity. When you realise just how much you want to be giving out, you will want to make even more money.

Another unwitting advantage is that people trust givers more because they believe you are not greedy. They are therefore more willing to give you opportunities.

4. Play a little

All work and no play leads to an early grave. As you make more money, it's okay to spend a little bit on nicer things. As long as you are saving a healthy amount, do some of the things you've never been able to.

This will keep you healthy, happy and motivated. Take your family on vacation – economy class. Buy new clothes. Hang out with your friends. Watch a game close to the action. Low-key things.

Let that fuel you to desire more.

Chapter 7: Grow your ambition

Over these few pages, you have learnt the importance of a side hustle for all income levels, the importance of your PDC and how to turn your side hustle into cheddar. There is so much more to learn, but you can pick that up from your mentor, other books, courses, and websites.

But I want to leave you with this final thought – grow your ambition. Don't stop wanting to do things bigger, better or easier. Keep striving for greatness. Be more excellent. If you can, grow a business from it.

It is not greed to want to grow your income tenfold or even a hundredfold. If you are spending wisely and giving a reasonable amount to good causes, then why not? I believe that as you grow and become wealthier, you will use what you have learnt to help other people do the same.

I'm not afraid of teaching people how to succeed and them making much more than I do. I would be proud if every reader of this book made ten times what I do! It means I am fulfilling my purpose in life.

My goal in life is to help one million people succeed. It's an ambitious plan, I know, but it is what keeps me going. Realising I am responsible for others challenges me to be better.

You might have different plans. Whatever they are, I encourage you to be ambitious. Grow your side hustle into a side flow. Be the next success story. Make yourself proud.

Don't let anyone tell you it can't be done, or there is a limit to your potential. If a man can become a millionaire picking up trash or cleaning toilets, you have a lot to hope for!

I won't promise the road will be easy, but it will be worth it.

I wish you all the very best!

Turn your passion into profit.
Love,
Manny

www.ingramcontent.com/pod-product-compliance
Lightning Source LLC
Chambersburg PA
CBHW030545220526
45463CB00007B/2988

ONE LAST THING...

I would really appreciate your feedback to my books and courses. If you enjoyed them, can you gift me your top marks so that it benefits other students?

If you found something that does not justify more than 3 stars, please, please let me know what exactly you want done or changed and I will make another video to reflect your views.

Happy Pips.

Paul Ardennes

Udemy course Instructor